For 150 years, St. Lawrence has been about programs that change lives.

For 150 years, St. Lawrence has been about discovering its place in the region ...and its place in the world.

For 150 years, St. Lawrence has been about people who cherish their roles as educators ...and people who cherish their education.

This book is published in honor of St. Lawrence University's Sesquicentennial celebration, connecting our past with our present to prepare for our future.

Since 1856, St. Lawrence has built its future upon the firm foundations of its heritage.

EDISON
ST. LAWRENCE UNIVERSITY

ST. LAWRENCE UNIVERSITY

Photography by

OTTMAR BIERWAGEN

Additional Photographs by Tara Freeman

Harmony House Publishers

Published by St. Lawrence University
In Conjunction With Harmony House Publishers
P.O. Box 90, Prospect, Kentucky 40059
502-228-2010

First Edition Printed in China 2006

Additional Photography by Tara Freeman

Executive Editors: Lisa Cania, Bill Strode
Design: Pat Propes

Library of Congress Number 2005934469
ISBN 1-56469-136-5

The new Student Center, immediately to the right of center, dominates this 2004 aerial view of the central campus.

Preface

When I was approached by the presidential search committee in the summer of 1995 about the possibility of returning to St. Lawrence as its president, my wife Ann and I were given a copy of the spectacular 1990 book of St. Lawrence campus photos. In it were both historic photos of the campus over the years and contemporary photos by photographer John de Visser. The St. Lawrence campus, in all seasons of the year, has always ignited in us powerful feelings of awe at its beauty. Looking at the photo book that summer of 1995 made us yearn to return and to make St. Lawrence our home once again.

As it happened, it fell to my presidency to address some long-standing issues of campus planning and facilities and campus landscape improvement—it was just time to tackle a great many issues and projects. So almost immediately the 1990 photo book was out of date in its representation of large areas of the campus and university buildings. The Owen D. Young Library and Dana Dining Hall were renovated; Brewer Field House was converted to what is now Brewer Bookstore; Appleton Arena was renovated to begin a whole series of improvements to recreation and athletic facilities and fields, including construction of the Newell Field House, Stafford Fitness Center, Leckonby Stadium, Sandy MacAllaster Field, Tom Fay Field, Creasy Way, the Robie Squash Center, North Country Field and the Merrick-Pinkard Track; the Steiner Senior Townhouses, the Wachtmeister Field Laboratory; and a new student center were constructed; renovation of the Edward John Noble Center for additional arts facilities was begun; and myriad smaller projects were undertaken, including many devoted to improving the campus landscape. Many new projects are in the late planning stages, including the first phase of our science and mathematics facilities project—a major new building for biology, chemistry, neuroscience and biochemistry—a major renovation of 76 Park St. (the small residence hall on Park St.) to become our new health and counseling center and new location for Security (allowing for the demolition and removal of the old bookstore and health center), and further stages of renovation and new construction in and around the Noble Center. In the last decade, the campus has been transformed again, as it was several other times in its history.

The confluence of that transformation and the University's sesquicentennial prompts this new book of photographs. We want to share with you the campus of today. Because it was our intent from the start, expressed in architectural design guidelines, you will see in the new a clear continuity with the best of our historic campus. I hope it reminds you too of home!

Dr. Daniel F. Sullivan
President
Fall 2005

A twenty-first century class is as likely to meet around a seminar table as in rows of chairs facing a lectern.

om

A ST. LAWRENCE CHRONOLOGY

PROLOGUE

Ca. 258 Archdeacon Lorenzo, later Saint Lawrence, is martyred on a giant gridiron for the crime of resisting civil authority.

1535 The French explorer Jacques Cartier sails into the estuary of a large North American river and names it for Saint Lawrence.

1802 The state Legislature creates St. Lawrence County; Canton, settled in 1801, is designated the county seat in 1828. Many of its early prominent citizens are Universalists.

BEGINNINGS

1856 Universalist Church leaders apply to New York State for a charter for a coeducational college of letters and science and theological school in Canton; the charter is granted to The St. Lawrence University on April 3, and the cornerstone of College Hall, now Richardson Hall, is soon laid.

1857 Ebenezer Fisher is named first president of the Theological School.

1858 The Theological School welcomes its first students.

1859 John Stebbins Lee is named first principal, or president, of the College of Letters and Science; Thomas Jefferson Sawyer is named first president of the corporation, a title eventually changed to chair of the Board of Trustees.

1861 Olympia Brown is accepted as a student at the Theological School; she graduates in 1863 as part of the first "TS" graduating class, and becomes the first American woman to be ordained a minister.

1865 Delos McCurdy and Hiram Ryel are the first graduates of the College of Letters and Science. Ryel may also be St. Lawrence's first graduate student; he receives his Master of Science degree in 1868.

1866 Sarah Elmina Sprague and Mary Cordelia Herrick are the first women graduates of the College of Letters and Science.

1868 Richmond Fisk becomes president; he also serves as chairman of the board.

1869 The first Moving-Up Day, then called Tree Holiday, is held. Enrollment stands at 46 and the comprehensive fee is $36.50.

1871 Herring Library, the second building on campus, opens.

1873 Absalom Graves Gaines becomes president; the P. D. Society, later to become a chapter of Beta Theta Pi, is the first fraternity at St. Lawrence.

1875 The Browning Society, later to become Kappa Kappa Gamma, is the first sorority.

1876 Scarlet and brown are designated the official school colors; the "Union Alumni Association" is founded.

1880 The first yearbook, entitled ***The Gridiron***, is published.

1886 "Town-gown" rally saves St. Lawrence from bankruptcy.

1887 E.A. Merritt is elected chairman of the board; he serves for 29 years, the longest term of office of any chair of the board. ***The Laurentian***, an alumni and literary magazine, is published for the first time.

1889 Alpheus Baker Hervey becomes president.

1892 First "modern" intercollegiate football game played.

1893 The first Freshman-Sophomore Debate begins the tradition of forensics competition at St. Lawrence.

1894 Poet Robert Frost visits campus to court his future wife, Elinor White, Class of 1895; the Thelomathesian Society becomes the official student government organization.

1896 John Clarence Lee becomes president.

1897 Emily Eaton Hepburn, Class of 1886, is elected to the Board of Trustees, the first woman to sit on this governing board.

INTO THE TWENTIETH CENTURY

1899 Almon Gunnison becomes first president of combined Theological School and College of Letters and Science; Lambda Chapter of Phi Beta Kappa is installed at St. Lawrence; first intercollegiate basketball season.

1900 Irving Bacheller, Class of 1882, publishes ***Eben Holden***, the first best-seller of the 20th century.

1902 Mary Young, hired to teach languages, is St. Lawrence's first full-time woman professor.

1903 St. Lawrence affiliates with the Brooklyn Law School, an affiliation which extends until the mid-1940s; Cole Reading Room opens as an addition to Herring Library.

1905 The "Great Rebellion" results in the suspension of 30-40 students. The "Rebellion" is begun after a student is reprimanded for smoking on the steps of Richardson Hall.

1906 The State School of Agriculture (later Canton ATC and then SUNY Canton) is founded on the St. Lawrence campus; Carnegie Hall of Science becomes the eighth building on campus. Enrollment is 194.

1911 *The Hill News* is founded as the official student newspaper.

1916 First telephone installed on campus, after much debate as to its cost-effectiveness.

1919 Ledyard Park Hale is elected chairman of the board; Richard Eddy Sykes becomes president.

1921 First Holiday Candlelight Service is held; the ***St. Lawrence Songbook*** is published.

1922 WCAD, one of the nation's first college radio stations, later to become KSLU, goes on the air at St. Lawrence; first "L" Club forms to honor athletes.

1923 First summer sessions are offered.

1924 Owen D. Young, Class of 1894, is elected chairman of the board; first alumni trustees elected; graduate program in education begins.

1926 Gunnison Memorial Chapel is built; first intercollegiate ice hockey season begins with a 1-0 loss to Clarkson.

1927 Dean-Eaton Hall opens as the first residence for women.

1928 First organized Alumni Fund is launched.

1929 Hepburn Hall for Chemistry is dedicated by Mme. Marie Curie.

1931 Men's Residence (popularly "Men's Rez", later Sykes Residence), opens as the first residence for men.

1933 The New York Giants play St. Lawrence's baseball team thanks to the influence of Hal Schumacher '33, later a star pitcher for the Giants for many years. Rev. Jeffrey Campbell is the first non-Caucasian to graduate from St. Lawrence.

1935 Laurens Hickok Seelye becomes president and establishes precursor of the First-Year Program; first of several joint St. Lawrence/Queen's University conferences on Canadian-American relations is held on campus.

1936 First "3-2" engineering program is instituted.

1937 The Outing Club is founded as the second collegiate Outing Club in the nation.

1940 Millard H. Jencks '05 becomes president.

1942 Edward John Noble is elected chairman of the board.

1943 Navy V-12 training program comes to campus.

1945 Eugene G. Bewkes becomes president; thanks to World War II, enrollment is 430, only 80 of whom are men. Professor Henry Reiff is a technical advisor at the San Francisco conference that creates the United Nations.

1946 The Laurentian Singers are founded.

1948 The State Education Department assumes control of the Agricultural and Technical Institute, formerly the State School of Agriculture.

1949 Howard McKinley '49 is St. Lawrence's first Rhodes Scholar.

1950 The men's basketball team defeats the Syracuse Nationals of the NBA; Appleton Arena is dedicated; its first event is a basketball game in January 1951. Enrollment is 1,445.

1951 Fisher Hall, home to the Theological School since 1881, is destroyed by fire.

1952 The Rovers, men's a cappella group begun in 1950, rename themselves the Singing Saints.

1953 The Sinners, women's a cappella group, are founded.

1955 Homer A. Vilas '13 is elected chairman of the board; Atwood Hall is dedicated as the new home to the Theological School.

1956 *Candle in the Wilderness: A Centennial History of St. Lawrence University* is published; Second Century Development Program gets under way.

1958 The David B. Steinman (later St. Lawrence) Festival of the Arts is inaugurated; first official telethon raises $4,950.

1959 Owen D. Young Library is dedicated; completion of Whitman Hall signals the start of a decade of residence hall construction.

1962 The University's first multi-million-dollar gift, from the Edward John Noble Foundation, funds the E.J. Noble University Center; St. Lawrence acquires the campus of Canton Agricultural and Technical College (ATC).

1963 Foster S. Brown '30 becomes president.

1964 St. Lawrence's first international study program, in Rouen, France, is established; the "Canton Creeper," the train that carried generations of students to and from Canton, ceases operation.

1965 Trustees vote to close the Theological School following the merger of the American Unitarian Association and the Universalist Church of America; St. Lawrence acquires Camp Canaras.

1967 The first computer is installed on campus, filling a classroom; study programs in Spain and Austria are established; Griffiths Arts Center, the campus' first dedicated arts space, opens.

1968 Arthur S. Torrey '24 is elected chairman of the board; WSLU-FM, later NPR affiliate North Country Public Radio, is licensed.

1969 Frank P. Piskor becomes president; the student-initiated Involvement '69 raises $20,000 for faculty development; Saturday classes are discontinued.

1970 The 4-1-4 calendar, featuring two full semesters and a short "Winterterm," is inaugurated; St. Lawrence students vote to strike classes for two days to protest the Vietnam War and the killing of four students at Kent State University.

1971 Augsbury Physical Education Center/Leithead Field House opens as the campus' first comprehensive athletics and recreation complex for both men and women.

1973 "Enterprise St. Lawrence - A Challenge to Enrich a Heritage of Quality and Independence" capital campaign is launched; St. Lawrence wins the national riding championship for the first of several times in the next decade.

1974 St. Lawrence's renowned study program in Kenya is launched as the first American college program in that country with a resident director; Washington (DC) Semester Program begins.

1976 St. Lawrence wins the national title in men's swimming.

1977 Study program in Canada is inaugurated.

1978 Alfred C. Viebranz '42 is elected chairman of the board; study program in London is established; ABC-TV televises a home football game nationwide.

1980 Enterprise St. Lawrence is completed with over $31 million in capital and annual funds accruing to the University; study program in Denmark is established; Torrey Wing of Owen D. Young Library is dedicated.

1981 W. Lawrence Gulick becomes president.

1983 John William Hannon Jr. '44 is elected chairman of the board; exchange program with Japan is started.

1987 Patti McGill Peterson becomes St. Lawrence's first woman president.

1988 All freshman students enroll in the Freshman (later First-Year) Program; St. Lawrence wins the national title in wrestling and competes in the national championship game in men's hockey; study program in the Soviet Union is begun.

1989 Exchange program with historically Black Fisk University begins. Enrollment is 2,097.

1990 Carnegie Center for International Education is dedicated; ODYsseus (electronic card catalog) is dedicated in the Owen D. Young Library; study program in India commences.

1992 Study program in Costa Rica begins.

1994 Launders Science Library created as part of renovations to Madill Hall.

LOOKING TO THE FUTURE

1996 Daniel F. Sullivan '65 becomes president.

1997 Study program in Australia is established; Canton Initiative, an effort to revitalize the community, is launched with a $1 million commitment from the University.

1998 Ten-year Master Plan for campus renovation and construction is announced.

1999 St. Lawrence wins the NCAA Division I men's soccer championship with the first perfect (undefeated, untied) season in American collegiate soccer history; study program in Trinidad & Tobago commences; University Fellows program gets under way.

2000 Study program in Florence, Italy, established; Adirondack Semester, based on international study programs, commences; Leckonby Stadium is dedicated.

2001 St. Lawrence's team plays in the first NCAA Division I women's hockey national championship game; Newell Field House and fitness center (later Stafford Fitness Center) is dedicated.

2002 Campaign St. Lawrence concludes with over $132 million raised or pledged; St. Lawrence hosts NCAA Division III men's soccer national championship tournament.

2003 Study program based in Shanghai, China, is established; special program in French-speaking countries for first-year students is launched; St. Lawrence hosts NCAA Division III track and field national championship meet.

2004 Student Center and Wachtmeister Field Station open; renovation of Noble Center and Griffiths Arts Center into an expanded and modernized arts facility begins; St. Lawrence hosts squash national championships.

2005 Sesquicentennial observances begin.

When it opened in 1857, College Hall (it did not become Richards
year, 1906) housed everything St. Lawrence needed, because it w

For nearly 80 years, the Bacheller Memorial Chime in Gunnison Memorial Chapel has, in the (adapted) words of the college song, "sung out the ending of each day."

versity's semi-centennial
ng on campus.

Close student-faculty interaction has long been a hallmark of a St. Lawrence education.

Research has become the watchword in science education in the twenty-first century.

With the first warm days of spring, classes head outside.

Coursework is not necessarily limited to campus. Gaines Professor of Psychology Tom Greene, an environmental psychologist, and his students engage in a research project on Canton's Main Street.

Inside classrooms and out (below, the Adirondack Semester yurt village on Massawepie Lake), students learn by working together.

A lab can be a room in a building, or all of outdoors.

What better time in life than the college years to call upon the creative muses?

The Laurentian Singers have been St. Lawrence's premier mixed-voice a cappella choir since just after World War II.

In the contemporary University, music-making blends art and technology.

The Singing Saints, seen here, and the Singing Sinners, male and female ensembles respectively, have been putting on entertaining shows—some of them impromptu–since the 1950s.

Known affectionately on campus as "tree houses," the top levels of each of the two-story study carrels in Owen D. Young Library have been popular with students since the opening of the Arthur Starratt Torrey Wing in 1980.

REFERENCE

One of the University's most cherished traditions, the Holiday Service of Lessons and Carols began in 1921 when several students "borrowed" some evergreens "of uncertain ownership," decorated the Theological School chapel, and put together an observance appropriate to the season.

The woods and waters of the nearby Adirondack Park have long attracted St. Lawrence students; the Outing Club, founded in 1937, is second only to Dartmouth's as the oldest collegiate outing club in the nation.

The Canoe House, busy with activity during the warmer months, reposes in the serenity of a winter's day.

Brewer Bookstore was for many years St. Lawrence's field house/gymnasium; when it was converted in the late 1990s, the original steel beams and the balcony over which students dangled their legs during basketball games (sometimes interfering with the opposition's strategy) were retained.

BREWER BOOKSTORE

GARDEN DESIGN
PAINT
Diarmuid Gavin

When it was built in 1931, "Men's Rez" (later Sykes Residence, in honor of Richard Eddy Sykes, Class of 1883 and president of the University, 1919-35) was the second dormitory on campus; Dean-Eaton Hall, for women, was constructed in 1926.

Memorial Hall.

Owen D. Young Library, Torrey Wing.

Herring-Cole Hall, second-oldest building on campus, and Herring-Cole Grove. Students planted trees here on "Tree Holiday," beginning in the 1860s, to bring some relief to what was then a barren former farm field.

Hulett (distant) and Jencks Halls.

The Student Center, opened in January 2004.

The Munro Family Climbing Wall in Newell Field House.

Interior of the Student Center.

The Steiner Student Residences, townhouse-style living for qualified seniors.

ALPHA TAU OMEGA

DEAN EATON HALL

Dean-Eaton Hall, with several students hoping the spring sun will come out.

Newell Field House.

Robie Squash Center.

The Ronald B. Stafford Fitness Center in Newell Field House offers 133 pieces of apparatus, as well as a varsity room.

St. Lawrence's men's and women's crew teams practice on the St. Lawrence River at sunrise.

North Country Field is an all-weather artificial turf facility that hosts men's and women's lacrosse and field hockey.

The women's basketball team advanced to the national championship game in 2002.

The men's soccer squad won the national championship in 1999, with the only undefeated and untied record in the NCAA history of the sport.

Softball became a varsity sport in 2000, and won the league title in its first season.

While most St. Lawrence teams compete in Division III of the NCAA, men's and women's ice hockey play at the "DI" level. The women's team (above) went to the Frozen Four in three of the first five years of its existence, while the men's team has appeared twice in the national championship game.

Sacrifice in Silence
Win out LOUD

SANDRZYK
22

The Saints Victory Bell, donated by her family and friends in memory of Katie Higgins '00 and presented to the University by her teammates on the 1998 women's lacrosse team, is rung jubilantly every time a Saints team wins a game.

Saints

SAINTS

80
10

NORTH COUNTRY
NORTH COUNTRY FIELD

Moving-Up Day is a spring Saturday dedicated to recognizing academic achievement and community spirit and to the symbolic "moving up" of each class, with representatives wearing gowns in their class colors.

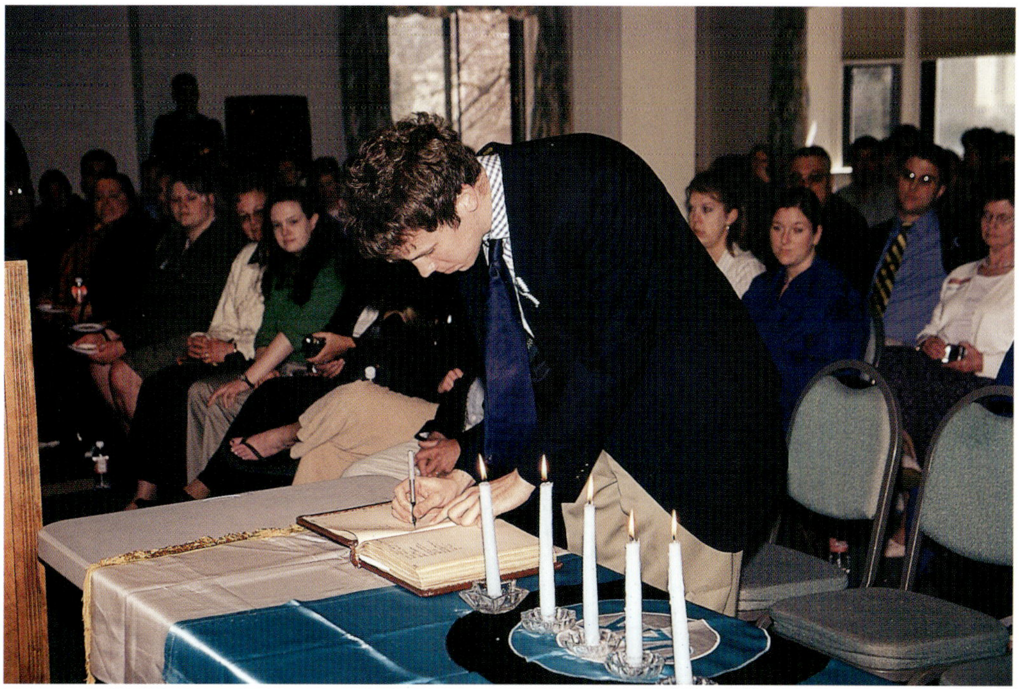

"Induction to Omicron Delta Kappa, the leadership honorary society (above) and Phi Beta Kappa, the academic honor society, are two cherished ways to recognize achievement."

Moving-Up Day includes the traditional "tapping" (along with a short run) for membership in Omicron Delta Kappa leadership honorary.

Commencement has proceeded outdoors, most recently on Creasy Commencement Commons, without stoppage for the occasional rain shower, or a famous 2002 snow flurry.

President Daniel F. Sullivan, the 17th president of the University when he took office in 1996, presents a diploma to a clearly pleased senior.

Reunion Weekend, customarily in early June, brings
Laurentians old and young back to campus.

'54
54

VNIVERSITAS SANCTI LAVRENTII IN NOV EBOR
ET
FIDES
VERITAS
MDCCCLVI

ST. LAWRENCE UNIVERSITY

150th Anniversary Retrospective

[College Hall (renamed Richardson Hall after the provider of a renovation in 1906) was the first and for some time the only building on the St. Lawrence campus. An 1857 calendar drawing calls it "the finest building in [St. Lawrence] County." It is listed on the National Register of Historic Places.]

Compiled by Neal S. Burdick '72 and Tracy L. Robertson, with the assistance of Lisa M. Cania M'82 and Kenneth D. Alger. Special thanks to the staff of the Vance Archives, Owen D. Young Library, and in particular Darlene Leonard, for locating and identifying many of these historic images.

top [Carnegie Hall, built in St. Lawrence's semi-centennial year, 1906, thanks to the philanthropy of industrialist Andrew Carnegie, was the first building on campus dedicated to science instruction.]

right [Science facilities took another step forward when Marie Curie (on landing) dedicated Hepburn Hall of Chemistry in 1925.]

right bottom [When Hepburn began to stretch at the seams after World War II, it was supplemented by space acquired when St. Lawrence purchased the state Agricultural & Technical College campus in 1962 and built Bewkes Hall (right in this architect's rendering) in 1968.]

[Gaines Open-Air Theater (seen here in 1926) was the site of Greek dramas, orations and other cultural events for many years. Named for Campbellina Woods Gaines, the wife of President Absalom Graves Gaines and a longtime beloved personality in University social and cultural life, it reposed approximately where Owen D. Young Library stands today.]

left top [St. Lawrence's first library was this room in College Hall; the collection consisted of a Bible, a few Greek classics and some days-old newspapers.]

above [With construction of Herring Library in 1870, St. Lawrence had its second building and its first intentional library edifice. Expanded with the addition of Cole Reading Room in 1903, it is listed on the National Register of Historic Places.]

left bottom [Owen D. Young Library ("ODY" to its friends) opened in 1959 with such modern amenities as a map room and study carrels. The façade seen here disappeared into the middle of the building when the Torrey Wing was appended in 1980.]

left [Laboratory work was added to courses in chemistry, physics and biology in the 1880s; at first, Prof. Henry Priest, who was the entire mathematics, physics, biology, astronomy and surveying departments in addition to teaching in other areas, made his own apparatus.]

above [St. Lawrence's music library, shown here in the 1980s in Griffiths Arts Center, was equipped with clunky tape recorders. Computerization and digital technology have created much more sophisticated facilities, as reflected in the 21st century's planned Arts Technology Center.]

26
6

left [For the first 25 years of its existence, the men's hockey team played outdoors, first on nearby frozen rivers and then on this rink, a flooded tennis court behind Dean-Eaton. Its first game was in 1926, against Clarkson (St. Lawrence lost), in what was to evolve into one of the most spirited rivalries in NCAA hockey annals.]

above [In 1951, Appleton Arena provided the team (and, many years later, the women's program) with an indoor home. The first event under Appleton's roof was a basketball game; it has also hosted graduations, trade fairs, car shows and rock concerts.]

ATHLETIC FIELD • ST LAWRENCE UNIVERSITY

Class of 1910

top [Weeks Field served as the University's earliest outdoor sports complex, with venues for football, baseball and track and field. This Word War I-era view shows the wooden bleachers that were later destroyed by fire, and the entrance whose design is perpetuated in today's Leckonby Stadium on the approximate site of the bleachers.]

far left [St. Lawrence's first dedicated athletics structure was the "Wooden Gym"; as shown here in 1897, women were from an early time expected to take part in physical education. The building burned under not very mysterious circumstances shortly before construction of Gunnison Memorial Chapel began on its site in 1926.]

middle [Brewer Field House quickly took the place of the Wooden Gym, and served as the physical education center and basketball venue for 45 years. After a long hiatus, it re-emerged as Brewer Bookstore in 1999.]

left [The opening of Augsbury Physical Education Center and Leithead Field House (rear) in 1971 marked a massive expansion of facilities for men's and especially women's sports, intramurals, recreation and fitness, as well as the end of a 20-year period of more or less constant construction on campus that saw the addition of 15 major buildings.]

[WCAD was to our knowledge the second campus-based radio station in America when it went on the air in 1922, with this comparatively primitive set-up in a corner room in Carnegie Hall. The station has been in continuous operation since, functioning today as KSLU.]

above [It was drafty and Spartan, but when just after World War II Laurentian Hall was erected on Maple Street of the recycled parts of an old Army gym, it was St. Lawrence's first student center, with space for plays, performances, meetings, social gatherings and a snack bar.]

right [Edward John Noble University Center, opened in 1962, was the University's first building put up for the specific purposes of a "student union," containing such features as the first true auditorium in St. Lawrence's 106-year history. This space in the basement was at times a game room, an eight-lane bowling alley (the hair styles and Fallout Shelter symbol on the post suggest that this view is from the late sixties), and a coffeehouse.]

[We do not know how many marriage proposals have been made on "The Wall" behind Dean-Eaton, seen here occupied by a significant percentage of the student body on a warm spring day in 1948.]

right [Dean-Eaton was St. Lawrence's first residence, although it was called a dormitory at the time; built in 1926, it was intended for women students, who had previously boarded in town. The tower belonged to the new radio station WCAD; behind it is the dairy barn on the adjoining campus of the State School of Agriculture, today's SUNY, Canton.]

below [Complementing Dean-Eaton, Sykes Residence was constructed in 1931 as the first men's residence on campus; in fact, that was its colloquial name, familiarly shortened to "Men's Rez."]

far right top [Whitman Hall was one of a series of dormitories constructed in the 1950s and 1960s, mostly along the campus' "Lower Road," to provide more adequate housing for a growing enrollment. To the consternation of some, it was later coeducational by wing.]

far right bottom ["Vetsville," the row of low structures in the top center, was erected to house the influx of students after World War II. Supposedly temporary, the barracks-like buildings remained in use for nearly 25 years.]

top [St. Lawrence began as first and foremost a theological school for the training of Universalist ministers. Until 1899, the Theological School (or "TS") and the College of Liberal Arts and Sciences—which became today's University—had separate administrations. When Fisher Hall was constructed in the 1870s, the "TS" also had its own building. It burned in 1951.]

top right [Atwood Hall opened in 1955 as the new home of the "TS"; when that school closed in 1965 upon the merger of the Universalist and Unitarian denominations, Atwood reverted to St. Lawrence, and has since housed the University's undergraduate and graduate education programs.]

bottom right [In the foreground are the buildings of the New York State Agricultural and Technical Institute, seen shortly before "ATI" moved to a new campus across town in 1962. St. Lawrence acquired ATI's facilities, and some of them remain in use today, among them Piskor and Payson Halls (left) and Valentine, Brown and Madill Halls (lower right).]

right [This is Richardson Hall—but not the one most Laurentians are familiar with. It was the home of Brooklyn Law School, in Brooklyn, N.Y., which for administrative reasons was an auxiliary enterprise of St. Lawrence from 1903 to 1945.]

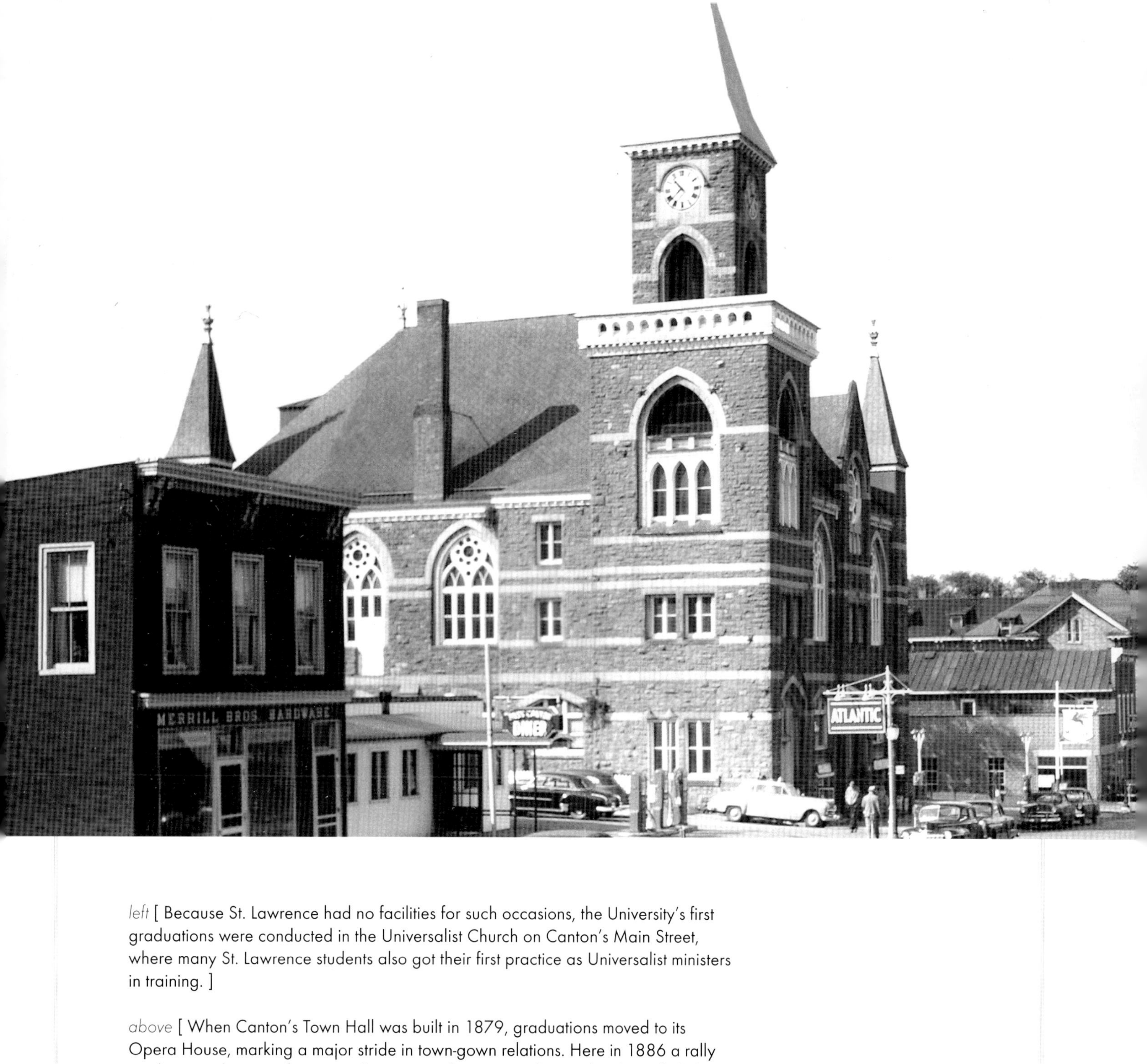

left [Because St. Lawrence had no facilities for such occasions, the University's first graduations were conducted in the Universalist Church on Canton's Main Street, where many St. Lawrence students also got their first practice as Universalist ministers in training.]

above [When Canton's Town Hall was built in 1879, graduations moved to its Opera House, marking a major stride in town-gown relations. Here in 1886 a rally involving students, professors and townspeople generated enough gifts and pledges to save the struggling University.]

top right [Gunnison Memorial Chapel, opened in 1926, provided the first adequate space on campus for graduation exercises. St. Lawrence had more than one Commencement ceremony a year for some time; this is the Summer 1949 event.]

above [As far as we can tell, 1950 was the first time St. Lawrence had an outdoor graduation; that year's ceremony took place on Weeks Field.]

left [Appleton Arena was the scene of Commencements for many years, alternating with Weeks Field; this is the 1974 occasion. In 1986, Commencements moved to a permanent outdoor location in front of the library, and Appleton has become a rain location that has never (through 2005) been needed.]

85
84
82
78

left [For many years, the alumni parade proceeded through town to the campus. Often, as in 1927, shown here, it coincided with Commencement Weekend.]

top [Another kind of town-gown interaction occurred when students occasionally appropriated community spaces for demonstrations of various kinds. This October 1969 protest of the War in Vietnam took place around the fountain in the village park.]

middle [For decades before the automobile caught on, the infamous "Canton Creeper" was the principal means by which St. Lawrence students traveled to and from home. Shown here is a Spring Break Special boarding in 1950. The depot, on Park Street between campus and downtown, was converted to a tavern after passenger train service ceased in 1964.]

bottom [The Sugar Bowl was a popular gathering spot in the center of downtown Canton for generations of St. Lawrence students, in the era before the University had an equivalent gathering place.]

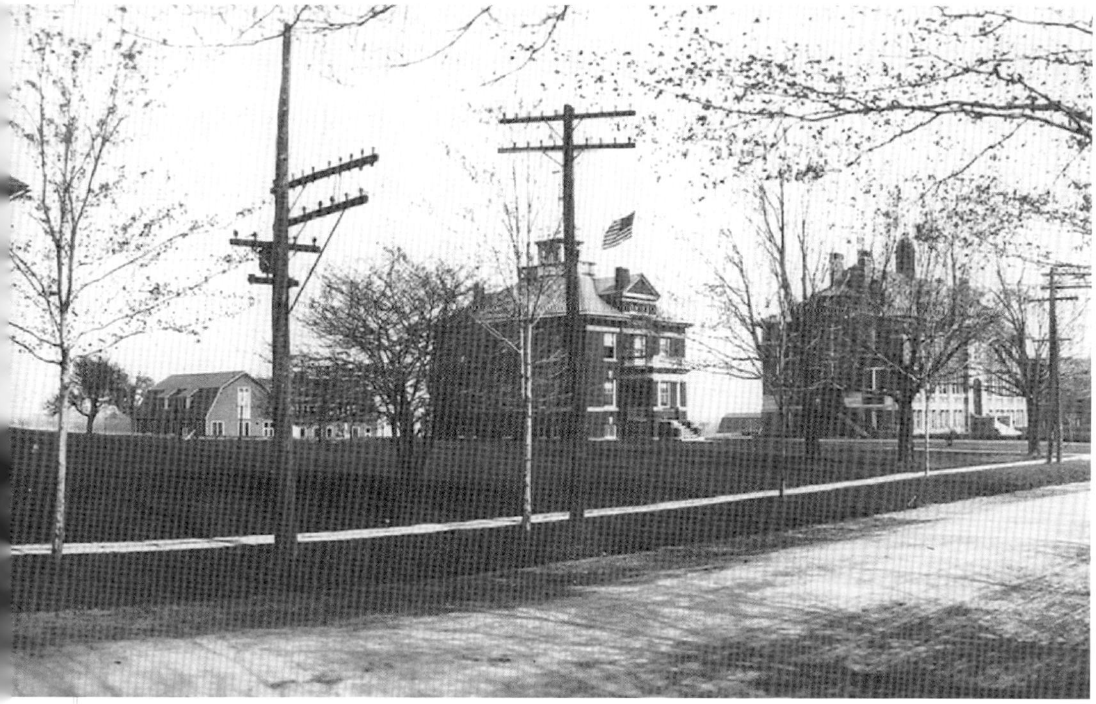

top [In the 1890s, the campus at age 40 contained four buildings: from left, College Hall, the Theological School's Fisher Hall, the President's House (partially hidden by Fisher), and Herring Library.]

bottom [By 1909, the campus had expanded to include not only the earlier Fisher and College Halls (far left) but also, reading right from College Hall, the Wooden Gym, Carnegie Hall and Beta Theta Pi, the first fraternity house on campus. The remaining buildings belonged to the state agriculture school; all but the barn in the background still (2005) function as part of St. Lawrence. They are Memorial Hall (which in 1909 housed a U.S. Weather Bureau station), Cook (now Piskor) Hall and Payson Hall.]

top [This aerial view of the campus in 1945 shows its expansion through the World War II era. The most dominant of recent buildings is Gunnison Memorial Chapel, which at the time was 19 years old.]

bottom [By 1972, the physical plant had grown even more, with such buildings as Hulett and Jencks residences, Griffiths Arts Center/E. J. Noble University Center and Vilas Hall (left to right, foreground) now part of the picture.]